# Desperate

## for God's

## Presence

# Desperate
## for God's
# Presence

## Understanding Supernatural Atmospheres

## Bill Vincent

Softcover 978-0615951430

PUBLISHED BY REVIVAL WAVES OF GLORY BOOKS & PUBLISHING

www.revivalwavesofgloryministries.com

Litchfield, IL

Printed in the United States of America

# Table of Contents

## *Chapter One*

# Changed by God's Presence

If I was to tell you that a moment in God's Presence could change your life forever. Everywhere we look, the Church is in desperate need to get a passion for God's Presence. After writing a five book series on the presence of God, I've learned that there is always more. No matter where you are in the things of God you need more of Him. I Pray that this book will cause you to hunger for what God has available in His Presence.

Does God still invade people's lives with the supernatural today?

What happens when God gets hold of a person? How is a person's life changed by a God encounter? Certainly, as Scripture shows, nothing is ever the same again!

Jacob's encounter with the living God—in a dream in the wilderness at Bethel—changed him from a deceiving plotter and trickster into Israel, "prince of God," and father of a nation of the people of God.

Moses' encounter with the living God—in a burning bush—changed him from a stuttering backcountry shepherd into a bold leader and deliverer of a nation who could confront the

Pharaoh of Egypt, the world's most powerful ruler.

Deborah's encounter with the fierceness of God changed a respectable judge into the deliverer of a nation who rendered courageous counsel to those in authority and vanquished the enemy's army.

Saul's encounter with the risen Christ—in a vision on the road to Damascus—transformed him from a fire-breathing persecutor of the Church into Paul, a fire-igniting apostle and evangelist who carried the gospel of Christ throughout the Roman Empire.

The archives of history also demonstrate that one God encounter can forever transform the course of a person's life.

Dwight L. Moody's encounter with the calling God—during a prayer meeting in a hay field—changed him from a poorly educated, unconfident shoe salesman into one of the greatest evangelists of modern times. He preached revivals across England and the United States where tens of thousands came to know Christ as Savior.

Kathryn Kuhlman's encounter with the relentless love of God changed an ordinary, red-headed, country girl into a world-impacting, miracle-working minister—all for the glory of God.

Billy Graham had an encounter with the Holy Spirit's empowering presence—over 50 years ago, in a hotel room in Los Angeles, California—and was thus transformed into one of the Church's all-time great evangelists who ushered hundreds of thousands of souls into the Kingdom of God.

Do you long for a genuine "God encounter" in your life? Do you wonder whether or not such experiences still happen today? Do you wonder whether it could happen to you? Then take heart!

God encounters do happen, and not just to "super-Christians." They also happen to ordinary people. How do I know? Because God encounters have happened to me. Believe me, if God encounters can happen to me, then they can happen to you. Cry out to Him and make yourself available to Him; He will not ignore you.

One word of caution, however: A God encounter changes everyone it touches. Once you receive the fire of God's visitation in your life, then you too will be forever changed. Let the presence of the Holy Spirit flood your being just as it has graciously impacted me. My own encounters with God set me free from fear and intimidation that had bound me all my life. During a supernatural encounter in prayer, God removed the "stronghold" that the spirit of intimidation had held over me since childhood. A God encounter happened in my life! I had always been very conservative and reserved and in a constant battle with intimidation. It made me sick, and I hated it. Much in me wanted to come out, but I seemed to have chains wrapped around my ankles. I was all bound up inside.

For years, I had cried out, "Lord, I just want to be so totally sold out and consumed with You that this fear gets completely defeated so I won't even have it anymore."

I thank God for hearing and answering my prayers. I've learned that God is jealous for a relationship with each one of us. He is angry at the enemy for clothing us with cloaks of comparison and intimidation that have nearly choked the life out of us. Today, God is standing up and warring on our behalf. He is setting the captives free and releasing us into the creativity He ordained for us from the beginning. This release applies to every area of our lives. It is time for us to set our own fashion standards. We weren't called to be like everybody else; we were called to be the unique person God fashioned us to be.

Many of us can't even walk across a room without wondering, what is everybody thinking about me? God's answer to such a mistaken mind-set is direct and to the point:

2 Timothy 1:7 For God hath not given us the spirit of fear; but of power, and of love, and of a sound mind.

1 John 4:18 There is no fear in love; but perfect love casteth out fear: because fear hath torment. He that feareth is not made perfect in love.

God has been wonderful to me. For years, He has been working on my intimidation and fear problems. Many who know me today would never have thought I had a problem with fear and intimidation.

Ester 2:9 And the maiden pleased him, and she obtained kindness of him; and he speedily gave her her things for purification, with such things as belonged to her, and seven maidens, *which were* meet to be given her, out of the king's house: and he preferred her and her maids unto the best *place* of the house of the women.

God wants to remove the old information that says, "You are unworthy." He wants to erase the old programs that taught you. He wants to remove the intimidation and compulsive comparison. God is saying, "Be yourself. I created you the way you are, and I love you just the way I made you." If you have sinned or failed in some way, then confess it to Him. He is faithful and just to forgive you. Do not be bound by mistakes of the past. If you have confessed the sin, then God has forgotten it, and you are clean before Him.

Intimidation will cause you to do what you would not do otherwise. When we are on the verge of a breakthrough, the enemy will attempt to come by surprise; he will try to intimidate us to make us settle for less than the total victory that we have yet to see. We need to press through, confront our enemy of intimidation, and allow the Holy Spirit's boldness to come upon us like the light shining through that gemstone. That light symbolizes the Word that is living and active, as it comes forth from within us.

We are all "living stones" precious in God's sight. As we stir up the gifts and callings within us and let the Lord's boldness come out, we will begin glowing like uncut gems in sunlight. We will become miracles visible to all. This is a good day to do business with God and decide to not let the enemy of intimidation strangle us anymore. It's time for every noose to come off and for us to bring out the gemstones to see the miracles that God wishes to do through us.

God wants to woo and draw you into His Presence. When He does, you will walk down that aisle to your Bridegroom with no shame on your face. You will be captivated by His love when He says, "Oh, how I've waited for you to come. How I've longed to embrace you and be in union with you." When you come into that place, all your fear just melts away. No matter how much the enemy tries to intimidate you, he can't stand before God's perfect love. Oh, how I love His presence and the embrace of my Bridegroom, Lover, and King. His presence is so great that it will change each one of us. We need to have confidence that our Father truly loves us. As a result, we will hear what the Lord will speak in days and nights ahead. We need to release the Holy Spirit's creative flow over everyone in our families and local church bodies. We need to be who God has made us to be. We need to let

Him saturate us with the "water" of His presence so that we can bloom, blossom, and release our unique fragrances. This will only happen as we look neither to the left nor to the right, but keep our eyes fixed on Him. We need to let Him set the standards of what we speak, how we act, how we dress, and how we live our lives. God has ordained that we live under His incredible banner of love, and beside that lies the fruit of His Kingdom presence. The word is here: No More Fear!

# *Chapter Two*

# Atmosphere of Miracles

When you talk about the Presence of God, you can't help but refer to atmospheres. The Lord has been speaking to me about healing and miracles in the atmosphere. I want you to listen for the voice of the Holy Spirit in the message in the Word of God, because I'm talking about how to receive healing in the atmosphere, and how you can take action or steps to being healed in obedience to God's Word.

Acts 14:8, 9 And there sat a certain man at Lystra, impotent in his feet, being a cripple from his mother's womb, who never had walked: The same heard Paul speak: who stedfastly beholding him, and perceiving that he had faith to be healed,

While Paul was teaching and preaching the Word of God, they brought a man that was crippled in both his feet, and he was born lame. As Paul was preaching the message, Paul was observing the man intently, seeing that the man had faith. I said, "God, what was the man doing? Was he jumping up and down?

12

Did he have a sign?" What was it about the man that Paul saw in the Spirit? In the Spirit, Paul saw faith. Paul was looking for faith.

I've been in meetings where people get into the prayer line. As I go down the prayer line, when I look at people, sometimes I can discern faith. It's a spirit of faith on them like an anointing. Other people are just without faith. You can feel that too. Faith is something you can see.

Act 14:10 Said with a loud voice, Stand upright on thy feet. And he leaped and walked.

Paul didn't even touch him. Paul looked at the man that was crippled in the wheelchair and said, "Stand up on your feet." Paul never touched him; Paul never prayed for him.

I've been in meetings where I've spoken the Word, the healing word, and someone would believe God with faith when hearing the Word of God. I'll say, "In the name of Jesus, take up your bed and walk," and someone will pick up their bed and start walking into their healing. Nobody prays for them, nobody touches them. What do you call that? It is the word for faith, and I call it a verb. It means action. Faith is moving, action. A lot of people don't have action in their faith. Let me give you an example.

There was a crippled man in the Bible with a withered hand. He wanted to be healed. Jesus said, "Stretch out your hand." The man stretched out his hand and he was healed. Jesus never touched him; Jesus never prayed for him. When the Lord said, "Stretch out your hand," he stretched out his hand. It was action.

It's like when Paul was preaching, he saw the man that was crippled had faith, so Paul said, without touching him, "Stand up on your feet."

I've been in meetings where people have had broken arms, and I would say, "Move your broken arm." They did not get healed until they moved their arm. You have to take a step of faith. Sometimes there are steps of action that you must take before you can receive your miracle. It happened many times when Jesus was preaching.

Mark 2:1-5 tells the story of a crippled man brought to see Jesus, but there were so many people they had to climb up on the roof. They opened up the roof and they lowered the man down. Jesus, seeing that the man had faith to be healed, looked at the him and said, "Take up your bed and walk." Jesus never touched him. You see, God is looking for faith. Paul saw faith. As he was preaching, he saw that the man had faith. All Paul had to do was say, "Stand up on your feet," and a man crippled from birth was healed.

I said "God, if I could get people into faith in my meetings, we could get people healed in the atmosphere. Just healed by taking a step of action."

Even while I'm preaching, I just say to you, "Move your legs, stand on your feet, and start walking." People just start moving, and the power of God shows up and begins to touch them.

There's a realm of healing and miracles that will not come without action; that will not come without steps of faith. Many times we have an excuse of why we cannot be healed, why God cannot give us a miracle, or why nothing has happened to us.

Kathryn Kuhlman said, "Faith is to stop believing in what you see, and start seeing what you believe."

Some of us have too much faith in what we don't see. Too much faith in what's happening in our bodies. Too much faith in what's happening in our circumstances. It's time to stop believing in what you see, the way that the doctor says it, and it's time to start seeing what you believe, what you believe in the spirit.

Why? Hebrews 11:1 Now faith is the substance of things hoped for, the evidence of things not seen.

You need to see yourself standing up; you need to see yourself whole and healthy. You need to see yourself leaping and dancing and running. You need to see yourself without pain. You need to see your miracle that's already happened in the spirit and receive it in Jesus' name.

The love of God, the sovereignty of God, heals people all the time that don't know Jesus. Some of the greatest miracles and healings that have happened in these meetings have happened to unsaved before they knew Jesus Christ. Why? Because of the love of God. The love of God and the sovereignty of God can heal.

I don't have a message that you must be in faith, but I'm saying when we get in faith, there's something that happens. God meets us and comes when He sees faith moving. Faith is a verb, faith means moving and action. Sometimes we've got to be willing to take that step. We've got to be willing to take that step just like when Jesus said to the crippled man, "Take up your bed." Jesus never even touched him; he just decided that he could be healed because Jesus spoke the word. He picked up his bed and walked.

The same with the man with the withered hand. Jesus said, "Stretch forth your hand." Or the story of the leper in the Bible, and the Prophet came to the leper and He said, "God's going to heal your leprosy. Here's what I want you to do. Go dip in the pool seven times. Until you go and dip in the pool seven times, you'll not be healed of leprosy."

There are things that we do sometimes that seem foolish and out of the box, unorthodox, and we don't understand. How is it that God couldn't just touch him, wave His hand over him and get him healed? Instead the Prophet said, "Go dip in the pool seven times."

I'm saying there are things that we need to do. That's why I tell people to put down their crutch and walk. Put down your cane and walk. Leave your walker and walk. Stand up out of your wheelchair on your feet. Take out your hearing aid. God will meet you. Sometimes you've just got to get people moving.

You have to get bold when praying for people in wheelchairs they've been in that chair for five years, or ten years, and they haven't used their muscles or their legs. When you pray for them, and they feel heat or electricity come in their body, then you say, "Stand up on your feet in the name of Jesus."

John 5:2-4, "Now there is in Jerusalem by the Sheep Gate a pool, which is called in Hebrew, Bethesda, having five porches. In these lay a great multitude of sick people, blind, lame, paralyzed, waiting for the moving of the water. For an angel went down at a certain time into the pool and stirred up the water; then whoever stepped in first, after the stirring of the water, was made well of whatever disease he had."

When there is an atmosphere and the Holy Spirit is moving, that's when we need to respond and do things. It's when the Holy Spirit is stirring and brooding and moving and hovering and vibrating.

When the presence of God is moving, we just start speaking things into the atmosphere, and people start coming to the altar. "I felt something happen in my body. There was heat in my body." People get healed in the atmosphere. You just need to get people moving. It also happens in worship.

If we're in the place of glory in worship, and I say, "Do something you couldn't do before," someone stands up in a moment of faith and they bend over and touch their toes. Their herniated disk is healed, their back is healed, their vertebra is healed, in the name of Jesus.

I believe faith is an anointing, I believe there's a gift of faith, a grace to have faith. Faith comes by hearing, and hearing by the Word of God. Faith is rising in our hearts to receive healing right now in the name of Jesus. That's why I tell people, "Put your hand on the part of your body that needs to be healed." There is currently a fresh Healing Awakening and season of Revival on earth. Take a step of Faith and receive your healing right now.

# *Chapter Three*

# Keys to an Encounter

E ncounters will help you stay in the perfect will of God. You and God can be connected just like Adam was in the beginning. It is time to find what keys help unlock God encounters?

God's Word tells us that a "three-fold cord is not quickly broken" (see Eccles. 4:12 KJV). This principle shows up throughout the Bible and in all of God's dealings with us. It should come as no surprise to find that God has given us three interwoven cords for unlocking His supernatural wonders in this life: faith; His manifest presence; and "imparters," or anointed and gifted people He places in our lives.

Faith is at the root of every blessing and work of God. Faith is of the heart; doubt is of the mind. In order to move in any dimension of faith, we need to engage our heart. The Bible reveals at least three degrees of faith.

The first category of faith comes at our "new birth." The moment we are born again in Christ, God gives each of us what the Bible calls "a measure of faith." This free allotment of faith must be exercised before it can increase (see Rom. 12:3-8). Our muscles

18

grow when we use, push, and exercise them. The same is true with our faith; if we exercise our faith it will grow strong. Each of us starts with a little bit—a measure of faith—but the more we exercise, the more we grow! A measure of faith is a beginning, but *only* a beginning—it is not the end. Faith is more than the key that unlocks the door to the Kingdom of God; as Christians, it is our very way of life. That is why we *must* grow beyond our new birth "measure of faith." We are born again by grace through faith. The born again experience enables us to see from the heart. A heart that can't see is a hard heart. Faith was never intended only to get us *into* the family. Rather, it is the nature of life in this family. Faith sees. It brings His Kingdom into focus.

All of the Father's resources, all of His benefits, are accessible through faith.

Faith of the second category comes through development. Every believer who yields to the Holy Spirit's continuous work in his or her life *will* bear spiritual fruit—it is inevitable and even mandatory.

This is part of the Holy Spirit's work of sanctification to mold us in the image and likeness of Christ. One fruit of the Holy Spirit that should rise up in our lives is "faithfulness" (see Gal. 5:22-23), which deals with God's character being revealed in our lives through trust and dependability. The Holy Spirit will develop honest, enduring fruit in our lives called faithfulness.

The third category of faith comes purely as a gift, which is why Paul called it the "gift of faith" in First Corinthians 12:9. It is a special surge of confidence in God and His Word that rises up in someone faced with a specific situation (see Mark 11:22-24). We could also call it "faith for the hour" because usually it does not manifest itself until needed. "Gift" faith can come to anyone who belongs to Christ, and that faith gets distributed as the Holy Spirit sees fit (see 1 Cor. 12:7).

Faith is a necessity for all of us; we cannot live life in the Spirit without it. Hebrews 11:6 states that without faith it is impossible to please God. On the other hand, Habakkuk 2:4b says, "But the righteous will live by his faith." This same verse is quoted three times in the New Testament: twice by Paul (Rom. 1:17; Gal. 3:11) and also in Hebrews 10:38. Faith is indispensable to our spiritual life and health and is a marvelous key for unlocking the supernatural in our lives. Faith comes (present active tense) and continues to come by the *rhema* words of Christ (see Rom. 10:17). Let us be people of faith in a supernatural God.

But remember, faith is always spelled one way: **R-I-S-K**. We must step out of our comfort zones to exercise our measure of faith.

The gift of faith can be expressed through words of faith spoken to God on behalf of a person, an object, or a situation. An Old Testament example is seen in the ministry of Elijah the prophet who spoke to God and, by faith, commanded the rain, the dew, and the end of drought (see 1 Kings 17:1; 18:41-45; compare this to James 5:16-18). Gift of faith can also be exercised in words spoken directly to a person, an object, or a situation on behalf of God. Joshua, for instance, spoke to the sun and moon on behalf of God (see Joshua 10:12-14). Many times, this happens when we receive the gift of faith to pray for a sick individual or for an apparently impossible situation. In the first instance, we would not only pray for the sick person, but also speak by supernatural faith, "Be healed in the name of Jesus." I have seen great things happen when the authentic gift of faith is in operation.

Supernatural faith was imparted to me through God encounters. Let faith arise, and watch as our enemies become like grasshoppers in our sight.

The second great cord in this rope of supernatural encounters is God's manifested (or openly revealed and tangible) presence among us. At times, the power of the Holy Spirit is especially tangible to perform signs and wonders in our midst.

Luke 5:17 says, "...and the power of the Lord was present for Him [Jesus] to perform healing." At another time, Jesus was walking in God's anointing in a crowd, but only a woman with an issue of blood had the faith to "plug into" the manifested presence of God and receive healing (see Mark 5:21-34, especially verse 30).

Other times, God imparts a "lingering" or resident measure of His Presence upon geographical regions where He did great things in the past; sometimes that impartation is even placed upon objects to set them apart for His own purposes.

The Bible tells of mourners who threw a man's dead body into Elisha's grave because some raiders were approaching. These mourners were shocked when their dead friend suddenly stood up alive after his body had come into contact with Elisha's bones (see 2 Kings 13:21). I would have loved to have seen that! Wouldn't you?

There are also what I call Holy Spirit "power points" in geographical regions, where God has released astounding supernatural power for His divine purpose.

One issue of faith must be settled for ourselves. We have all heard ministers say, "Oh, the anointing is strong here." That's great! But through faith, we must learn to tap into the strength of anointing that lives within every one of us born-again believers; Christ, the Anointed One, does live within us. We must learn to draw from the "well of salvation," that anointing of His presence within us, and bring it (actually Him) forth to give cups of His presence to those around us.

The third cord in our three-strand rope of supernatural encounters is the ministry of "imparters." Near the beginning of his letter to the Romans, Paul wrote, "For I long to see you in order that I may impart some spiritual gift to you, that you may be established" (Rom. 1:11).

Paul was an "imparter," a gifted servant of God used to share, impart, or pass along what He had given him. Paul told his young disciple, Timothy, "I remind you to kindle afresh the gift of God which is in you through the laying on of my hands" (2 Timothy 1:6). Earlier in his life, Paul (then known as Saul) was the recipient of what Ananias had imparted to him (see Acts 9:17).

In the Old Testament, God used Moses to impart an anointing for leading Israel into Joshua (see Deut. 34:9); and Elijah imparted a double mantle of the prophet's anointing to Elisha (see 1 Kings 19:15-21; 2 Kings 2:1-12).

Even the strong-willed King Saul was transformed (temporarily) into "another man" while under the influence of God's prophetic presence upon others (see 1 Sam. 10:5-12; 19:20-24). Even today, God continues to use imparters to attach us with spiritual "jumper cables" and recharge the weakened batteries of our lives.

We must have compassion to move in the powerful, super-natural presence of God. Our heavenly Father—who always demonstrates His compassion toward us—imparts compassion to us that we might demonstrate it toward others.

The Holy Spirit wants us to have God's heart on a matter, so as to release an expression of compassion through us. Have you been stirred within and find yourself bursting to see God break through?

God's will and word are paramount in all demonstrations of Holy Spirit ministry. No matter what activity of the Spirit we see, or are involved in, it must match up and conform to God's revealed will as outlined in the Bible (see 1 John 3:21-24; 5:15). What does God's Word say?

What is His revealed will? We *must* apprehend this knowledge, if we are to move out in the anointing with confidence.

What time is it? Has God's strategic timing come for the release of this activity? The Lord often releases supernatural signs at just the appointed moment—and not before.

The Greek New Testament uses a number of different words that translate into the English word "time." *Chronos* and *kairos* are the two most significant meanings of time. *Chronos* refers to a sequential order of time—a chronology—while *kairos* refers to a specific strategic moment, such as when Paul speaks of "the fullness of the times" for "the summing up of all things in Christ" (Eph. 1:10). What time is it? Has the *kairos* appointment of God's calendar appeared?

We also must be sensitive to the Spirit of God. It is no accident that the Word of God says, "And the spirits of the prophets are subject to the prophets" (1 Cor. 14:32 KJV). This means that we don't have to "blurt out" everything revealed by God at the very moment He speaks to us. He is not the author of confusion; He knows exactly when and how our particular piece of the supernatural puzzle fits into place, and He will work within His established authority structure (see 1 Cor. 14:33).

We should always ask ourselves, "When does God want this supernatural act demonstrated or word released, and why?"

We have prepared ourselves to receive supernatural revelation from God. Once that revelation came, we examined ourselves, our source, and the content of our message. We have been careful to fit into God's plan, purpose, order, and timing. Now, how do we release the supernatural? Part of the answer can

23

be found in ministries of those who have gone before us.

First Samuel 16 describes the day when the prophet Samuel was sent to anoint the son of Jesse in backwater Bethlehem. The problem was that Jesse had many sons—eight, in fact. Samuel was full of God's anointing and his ram's horn was filled with anointing oil. He was all set to go, except that he didn't know upon whom to release that oil. He couldn't trust his natural instincts— God had already warned him about that (see 1 Sam. 16:7). Even though he didn't know everything, Samuel knew enough to get him going. Often, we don't get more information until after stepping out in faith with what little we already possess.

Samuel assumes that the firstborn son is the one to receive the anointing. After all, the firstborn had the birthright, so that makes it a logical assumption. Samuel proceeds to begin anointing Jesse's oldest boy, but the Holy Spirit stops him. Through years of ministry, I have found that we need to do what Samuel did in this situation. He prayed through all seven sons, but still the Spirit did not say, "This is the one!" Finally, Jesse pulled David—the forgotten eighth son—out of the fields and, at last, God allowed Samuel to release His anointing.

Remember, we tend to look on the outward appearance, but God looks on the heart. In times of strategic decision-making situations, it is especially important to pray through all choices that are present. Let each one pass "under the rod" of God's discernment and anointing! Have faith in God. He will confirm the one(s) whom He chooses!

Another model of ministry is found in the patient life of Simeon. We need to have eyes like those of Simeon, the aged saint who won God's promise that he would live until seeing the anointed Messiah with his own eyes (see Luke 2:25-35). Simeon fervently sought God until receiving a divine promise of supernatural revelation. Then, he continued in patient "waiting and watching" until his promise came to pass. At that point, Simeon confirmed—with divine authority in the Spirit—what had taken place and painted a prophetic picture of what was to come.

We, like Jesus, are to do what we see the Father doing (see John 5:19). Have you waited on the Lord? Have you been watching to see what He might speak to you? May the Holy Spirit open the eyes of our heart and grant the "seer" grace so that we can do the works of Christ.

God often uses "imparters" as Holy Ghost "fire starters" and "point people" who pioneer new vistas, outreaches, and growth in the Spirit. Their principal purpose is to get others going, to equip them for God-ordained tasks, and then to turn them loose. Our central goal is to see the multiplication of God's glorious presence in the earth.

Lord, light the fire again! Raise up Your true champions of the faith who carry a torch for their generation to impart to others.

Generally, we can measure the value that people put on something by the amount of patience exhibited when trying to acquire it. Although people are often unwilling to stay very long in a church service, they will gladly spend the night waiting to get tickets for the Super Bowl or the World Series! God knows our frame of mind (see Ps. 103:14). He knows that when we practice the godly attribute of patience solely to capture His presence, then we have placed a great value on what is nearest to His heart. Patient waiting draws the Spirit's presence to us. Waiting is a magnet that woos His coming.

Even a casual reading of the Gospels reveals that worship was the attitude and posture of many who came to Jesus for a supernatural touch. They often bowed down in reverent worship before making and receiving their request. As you wait upon the Lord and worship, let your faith go up to Him and expect great things!

He loves to bless those who anticipate great results from Him by faith. Waiting expectantly and worship fit together like a hand in a glove.

We have looked at some keys to the supernatural, but are there ways of wisdom to be learned here also? Divine revelation is like a pot of boiling water on a stove. We need to put on mittens of wisdom to carry the pot to a place of usefulness and purpose. Otherwise, we will spill the contents all over ourselves! If we mishandle divine revelation, we will end up getting burned. Every gift and revelation of God in our hands is like a loaded weapon or powerful medicine—if handled unwisely, it can hurt and destroy instead of healing and building up.

If we discern a problem in a certain situation and fail to seek God's wisdom, our gift of discernment can become a tool of gossip that destroys the lives of others. Remember Proverbs 12:8: "A man will be praised according to his insight...." Ask for God's "insight with wisdom and understanding."

## *GETTING STARTED*

1.     When you have received revelation from God for some-one else, turn the words into a question as you present it, such as "Does this mean anything to you?" Be humble in your approach, and do not act like a "know-it-all!"


2.     Turn your revelation into intercession. Pray the inspiration, instead of sweating out heavy perspiration. Pray the promise back to God!

3.      Submit your impressions (revelation) to trusted counsel. God will not give all of it to you anyway. Trust Him to speak through others as well.

4.      Realize that if you have received the genuine article, then a natural tension comes along with it. You may ask your-self, "Do I sit on this or run with it?" This tension is a normal part of your learning curve. He will teach you what to do!

5.      Learn the lesson quickly and well from Proverbs 29:11a (KJV): "A fool uttereth all his mind." Don't be a fool. Ask the Holy Spirit questions, and also watch and learn from others for answers to these questions: "What do I say? To whom do I give it? When do I release it? Where do I present it?" Most of us learn this proverb by experience!

6.      As you grow in gifting, eventually another situation will arise: You will be praised because of your (His) gift. What do you do with these trophies that people bring to you?

Learn to respond wisely to "second heaven revelation." Not every revelation you receive is a declaration of what is sup-posed to come to pass. At times, the Holy Spirit may give you insight into one of satan's schemes. Don't be alarmed; Paul said we are not to be ignorant of the devil's schemes (see 2 Corithians 2:11). "Second heaven revelation" refers to information received concerning the enemy's evil plans. God gives these insights to enlighten and forewarn us, so we can either prepare or eliminate it through intercession. God's will and plan will determine which option to use.

Be careful with your curiosity. Is the Holy Spirit leading you into this new experience? Are your soulish desires or divine initiative in charge? Are you being led by your passion for Jesus or is an enticing spirit leading you toward darkness? Many people have found themselves drawn toward the occult—supposedly for the purpose of "learning the enemy's devices"—and end up entangled in deception. The fruit is distinctly different: With an enticing spirit, you end up "beat up" and discouraged; when God is your guide on a supernatural journey, He leaves you enlightened and empowered.

Always give your revelation with gentleness (see Gal. 6:1; 2 Tim. 2:23-26). The wisest path is to minister in humility. Hard confrontation is the exception, not the norm. If your revelation involves rebuke or correction, go through the standard procedures of first speaking, second exhorting, and third warning with all authority—as according to the biblical pattern in Titus 2:15: "These things speak and exhort and reprove with all authority. Let no one disregard you." Gentle-ness and humility disarm fear and build the bridge that allows the cargo to cross.

Realize that some words are conditional, and some revelations are given without any condition being spoken. Consider God's word to Jonah about Nineveh being destroyed in 40 days. Was the city destroyed? No, because the people of Nineveh took God's prophet seriously and repented. Jonah was tried himself by the revelations God gave him. But, eventually, God showed him the true purpose of His pronounced judgment: restoration and compassionate redemption (see Jon. 3:4–4:11). Behind every word of judgment stands a merciful God ready to forgive. Again, consider the example of Amos 7: The prophet was given five visions of judgment, and all of them were true revelatory experiences. Yet Amos' inter-cession blocked two of the five prophecies from coming to pass! Again, this is an example of a merciful God!

Make sure that your revelatory ministry is saturated with mercy and grace and not haughty pride. Wisdom shouts the fear of the Lord (see Prov. 9:10). Never use your revelation as a tool of punishment.

The Holy Spirit once spoke to me, "Be careful not to stretch the rod of your mouth out against the House that the Lord builds." Work with God, and not against Him and His appointed leaders. Put on the fear of the Lord. Don't borrow and snatch! Avoid using another person's revelation as your own just to gain credibility before man. If necessary, ask the other person for permission to restate his or her prophetic word, and then give proper credit. When asked about another person's word, stand secure and simply say, "I don't know. You will have to consult him." Avoid being tainted by an evil report; you can become soured on a person by listening to another speak evil about him, all under the guise of revelation. We all need to read and learn the truths found in chapters 13 and 14 of the Book of Numbers.

Then, we need to be cleansed by the blood of Jesus from the defilement of evil reports and gossip. Remember, it's the gift of discerning of spirits—not gossip concerning another's problems. Be alert to the activity of the "accuser of the brethren."

Satan seeks every opportunity to spew his filthy stew of accusation on believers (see Rev. 12:10). Peter warned us, "...be on the alert. Your adversary, the devil, prowls about like a roaring lion, seeking someone to devour" (1 Pet. 5:8). Fall out of agreement with the devil! Speak, release, and declare the medicine of life into broken situations. Do not throw away your personal relationship with God. No matter how high the level of prophetic activity gets around you, never depend primarily on the "ears" of others. The Spirit of God dwells within you, so you must hear God for yourself!

Read chapter 13 of First Kings (especially verse 1) concerning an intense account of prophetic activity. Get your own revelation from God; do not let someone else hear for you. Hear God for yourself first, and then let Him use others to confirm what you heard!

## DON'TS OF SUPERNATURAL MINISTRY

1.        Never allow what you hear through others to become a substitute for hearing the Holy Spirit's voice for yourself. This also means never allowing revelations heard coming from men to override your devotion to the Scriptures (see 1 Kings 13). God is a jealous God (see Exod. 20:5). He wants you to spend time with Him! Stick to the basics!

2.        Never lift up a vessel who brings the Word of God. Lift up Jesus! Remember, the testimony of Jesus is the spirit of prophecy (see Rev. 19:10). Let Jesus truly be the chief prophet in our midst! Remember God's solemn warning in the Book of Isaiah, "And My glory I will not give to another" (Isa. 48:11b). We live in an age of mercy and grace, but God has drawn clear limits where His glory is concerned.

3.        Don't be naive. "The naive believes everything, but the prudent man considers his steps" (Prov. 14:15). Do not believe every spirit! Test the spirits to see if they are of God (see 1 John 4:1-6). Ask for wisdom (see James 1:5; Ps. 25:4).

4.        Don't twist the meaning of the revelation to comply with your desires, wishes, hidden agenda, mixed motives, timing, or aspirations. Hold onto the words with open, "no-strings-

attached" expectancy that our supernatural God will fulfill His words in whatever manner He chooses. Don't treat prophetic experiences as taffy that can be pulled and stretched to fit your desires.

5.    Don't quench the Holy Spirit. First of all, do not "despise prophesyings" (see 1 Thess. 5:19-21 KJV). (Some people with a revelatory ministry mysteriously don't want to receive or acknowledge prophecies from anyone else!) Counterfeit prophecies and mixture do occur, but don't be disillusioned. Keep in mind two ditches to avoid: despising or disdaining the supernatural, and becoming excessively fascinated or enamored with it. But don't let failure stop you! Believe God for His full restoration of pure prophetic ministry. It is worth the journey.

## DO'S OF SUPERNATURAL MINISTRY

1.    Earnestly desire the Holy Spirit's gifts. In the words of the apostle Paul, "...desire...especially that you may prophesy" (1 Cor. 14:1). Not only does God want to speak to you, but He also wants to speak through you! Desire the gift of prophecy!

2.    Believe God's prophets and you will succeed (see 2 Chron. 20:20). Rejoice! What a privilege you have been given. All you have to do is mix faith with God's words and receive His results. But always remember to place your faith in the God of the Word, and not in the man of the word.

3.    Pray the promise back to God. Follow Daniel's example of respectfully and humbly reminding God of His word through intercession (see Jer. 29:10; Dan. 9:1-19). Bathe the

prophetic invitation in prayer.

4.     Fight the good fight. Use the spoken *rhema* word of prophecy in your life as equipment for spiritual battle (see 1 Tim. 1:18). Do spiritual warfare against discouragement, doubt, unbelief, and fear through declaring the prophecies given over your life.

5.     Seek confirmation at all times. Remember the biblical measure of validity: "Out of the mouth of two or three witnesses every fact is to be confirmed and established" (see Deut. 19:15; Matt. 18:16; 2 Cor. 13:1). Walk with others and seek the mind of Christ through godly counsel.

Generally, the Church has two types of ministries: the "shooting star" and the "north star." A shooting star rises fast, blazes bright, and draws much attention with its flashy ministry. But it burns furiously for a short time, and then quickly fades through moral failure or a fatal character flaw. On the other hand, the "north star" ministry is fixed, stable, and consistent; it may not be as flashy, but it's used for generations to give guidance to those on the seas of uncertainty, and it does so without wavering or wallowing in sin. People with a "shooting star" ministry seek a single anointing; they go for the fullness of God's power without waiting for the fullness of God's character. Character does involve waiting because it must be "grown" into us through experience and countless small and great acts of obedience. "Shooting stars" pay virtually nothing up front, but they pay dearly in the end. Believers with a "north star" ministry make the best choice. But they "pay the cost" every day by taking up their cross, following Jesus, and obeying His commands every step by painful step. They have submitted themselves to God's will so that they may be "conformed to His image." As a result, they earn a double anointing of the fullness of God's character and power in their lives. That is how we develop "the character to carry the gift."

God is going to continue pouring His living waters into each of us to flush away the hurts, bitterness, and debris that we try to hide. He is determined to make us into vessels that contain His glory. In our pursuit of keys to God encounters, let's cooperate with the work of the Cross in our lives so that we might have character to carry the gift. To be one who releases His contagious presence.

## Chapter Four

# Love Casts Out All Fear

It's been burning in me for a while that the Church as a whole has lost its love for one another. The Church has been destroying itself by self-destruction. I will barely touch the surface here but expect more in another book. FROM THE BEGINNING OF TIME God planned to mightily strengthen you in these last hours. Before you were even conceived, He knew that He would be giving you a miraculous breakthrough over fear through a new dimension of relationship with His Son. This is a relationship that is founded and rooted in the power of love, a love so powerful that it has overcome the entire world and every unclean spirit in it! God tells us, *"There is no fear in love; but perfect love casteth out fear: because fear hath torment..."* (1 John 4:18). This is a dynamic passage of truth. Before we go any further, let us look at the Amplified Bible's translation of this verse in its entirety. It says:

1 John 4:18 There is no fear in love; but perfect love casteth out fear: because fear hath torment. He that feareth is not made perfect in love.

Take a moment now to reread this passage. Allow it to penetrate deeply into your spirit. For this takes us right into the heart of the reason why some of us fail.

We have read the phrase, "perfect love casts out fear," so many times that we have assumed it is always Jesus's love for us that is to do all of the work. However, there is another way of looking at this. Remember that we are in a covenant relationship with our Lord and with each other. It is a covenant of love, and love is a two-way street. Therefore, not only is it Christ's powerful love for us that casts out fear, but our love for Him should cause us to stand up in union with Him and literally kick that spirit of fear right out the door!

Think about it. When you truly love someone, and become one with them, you love what they love, and hate what they hate. Our relationship with the Lord is no different. Through His Word we are told, *"Ye that love the Lord, hate evil..."* (Psalms 97:10). There is no worse evil than fear. This being the case, all of you who truly love Him will fervently desire to no longer tolerate all of those fears that are so offensive to Him. You will no longer put up with those vile, fearful thoughts which so brutally block your communion with Him. From now on, you will rise up and refuse to let any fear pollute your heart and mind. As soon as you take this stand, something dramatic will begin to happen. You will come into an even deeper revelation of His love for you! The cry of your heart will change. Instead of it being a constant plea for deliverance, it will be, *"...that I may know Him [that I may progressively become more deeply and intimately acquainted with Him]..."* (Philippians 3:10 AMP).

And know Him you will. You will come to know Him in a deeper way each time you choose to let your love for Him rise up and, with Him, expel those fears right out of your mind. He will then rush in to fill all of those areas where fear once dwelt, and you are one step closer to being totally restored.

By now you may be saying, "What can I do? I don't have that kind of love for the Lord yet. I want to, but I'm not quite there."

Let me help you. Know that He is right there with you, knocking at the door of your heart, longing to come in (see Revelation 3:20). The only problem is that you don't know how to come into the experience of His Presence. You don't know how to open the door. To help you discover where the blockage may be, sit down and ask the Holy Spirit to lead you through the following questions:

• Do I really crave and desire His Presence more than anything else in the world, no matter where I am or what the circumstances are?

• Do I take the time each day to meet with Him, to spend time with Him, time when I'm not begging for anything or dictating to Him but just being still before Him in adoration and worship?

• Do I raise my voice to Him, singing to Him in my heart, praising and thanking Him continually, or do I withhold it because I'm afraid?

• When He asks me to do something, what is my response, and how quick is it?

• Am I totally willing to relinquish my fears (which I have become so accustomed to), so that I might dwell quietly in His peace?

• Do I get so caught up in the cares and works of this world that I postpone devoting myself to a relationship with Him?

• Does He mean more to me than my reputation, the opinions of others, my family, my possessions, or my ambitions, even my ambitions for Him?

• How much does obedience to Him mean to me? Have I completely given Him my will? What price am I willing to pay?

- Do I have any unpaid vows?

Whatever that price is, please do not be afraid. Make up your mind now that you are willing to pay it.

# Chapter Five

# Moving in the Supernatural

In the Supernatural realm there is a protocol of how you operate. Anyone beginning to walk in supernatural realms of God soon discovers one of the biggest challenges is learning how to "go with the flow." We want to swim with the Holy Spirit's current and not against it, so as not to quench, or even shut off, His anointing. As with any other spiritual discipline, there are principles to this process.

When learned and practiced, these keys greatly facilitate the art of stepping into prophetic currents and moving with the supernatural flow.

The Scripture passage from the fourth chapter of Second Kings illustrates several key principles for flowing in prophetic power of the supernatural. A desperate mother—the widow of one of the "sons of the prophets"— seeks Elisha's help because a creditor is coming to enslave her sons since she cannot pay her debt. The only valuable item that this poor, destitute woman has is a small jar of oil. Remember that oil is a common biblical symbol for the Holy Spirit. Under Elisha's direction, she borrows many large containers from her neighbors and, in private with her sons, pours oil from her jar into the containers. The oil continues to flow until every container is full, and then stops. By selling the oil, the woman can pay off her debt, and she and her sons can live on the rest of the proceeds.

A great key for moving in the supernatural flow is investing in the next generation. In this passage, the woman is known as the widow of one of the "sons of the prophets." At that time, there were prophets, and sons of the prophets, and this helps us to understand the trans-generational anointing. I'm not necessarily talking about ages here, although that is important.

We have a responsibility to give away what we have to those younger than us; that way, we can help raise up the next generation of Spirit bearers. The key, however, is not to focus on age so much as to look for good quality soil, and then sow into it liberally.

In any period of time, two or three generations coming together—in a divine junction—produces a holy interaction that greatly multiplies the anointing. Just as God does not give His revelatory graces for one person alone, neither does He give them for one generation alone. Each generation of anointed, prophetic people have a responsibility to invest in the next generation, who are the sons of the prophets.

The second principle for moving in the supernatural flow is bringing what you have. Elisha asked the widow, "What do you have in the house?" All she had was a small jar of oil, so that is what she brought, and that is what the Lord used to bless her. To move in the supernatural, you must start in the natural by sacrificing, giving freely, and lavishing God with whatever you already have.

How much or how little is not the issue; what matters is having a heart of faith, surrender, and obedience. Even our lack, when coupled by faith in God's provision, becomes more than enough. Remember the story of the widow's mite in Mark 12:41-44, where Jesus draws a lesson from watching people contribute to the temple treasury:


Mark 12:41-44 And Jesus sat over against the treasury, and beheld how the people cast money into the treasury: and many that were rich cast in much. And there came a certain poor widow, and she threw in two mites, which make a farthing. And he called *unto him* his disciples, and saith unto them, Verily I say unto you, That this poor widow hath cast more in, than all they which have cast into the treasury: For all *they* did cast in of their abundance; but she of her want did cast in all that she had, *even* all her living.


Jesus makes it clear that the value of this poor widow's gift was not in its monetary amount, which was insignificant, but in the faith behind it. Others gave "out of their surplus," which was what they could spare. But this widow put in her last two coins, which was "all she had to live on." Such an act reveals her knowledge that God was her true source and also shows her faith in His provision. Likewise, the widow of Second Kings chapter 4 invested everything she had. She willingly gave up her jar of oil and received it back multiplied a hundredfold or more. By giving what she had, she released God's power.

Elisha told the widow to borrow empty vessels, and not a few. The oil of the prophetic anointing must have a container into which it can be poured. Like the widow's jar of oil, God's anointing is flowing and can fill up as many vessels as are available and ready. The greater the number of vessels, the greater the blessings that flow—it is a simple principle of multiplication.

First, the widow had to borrow empty vessels. God is also looking for empty vessels: people empty of self who will pour out themselves for God; people who have passion for God and will have compassion for people.

Empty vessels are ripe for blessing because God can fill them up with Himself in undiluted measure. This image is similar in concept to Jesus' words on the Sermon of the Mount: "Blessed are the poor in spirit, for theirs is the kingdom of heaven…Blessed are those who hunger and thirst for righteousness, for they shall be satisfied [filled]" (Matt. 5:3,6).

Second, the widow was to get "not a few" vessels, but to bring as many as she could get her hands on. This activity of multiplying anointing is not for a few, but for the many.

God's revelatory power graces are not elitist; I want to shatter this small-minded mentality in the Church that believes God's supernatural power is for an elite group. Moving in the super-natural flow is for as many who will make themselves empty vessels and come to the Lord for filling. A consequence to this fact is the importance of acquiring a big vision. Imagining many vessels being filled with God's anointing requires big vision. Don't limit yourself, or the Lord, by thinking too small. Your measure of anointing and your degree of blessing are limited only to the size of your vision.

How do you know if God has planted an idea in your spirit? Does your vision involve something that only God can accomplish? If so, then He is the One who put it there; God speaks to us about what we cannot do.

If these visions are to come to pass, then He will have to perform them. God does not inspire us to attempt what we can do on our own; if so, then we would not need Him. Instead, He speaks to us of what we cannot accomplish so that we will reach upward to Him. God is not only about accomplishing vision, but is also about drawing us into Himself.

After gathering as many empty vessels as she could, the widow had to shut the door and be in private with her two sons. One key to moving in a supernatural dimension is learning to cultivate a hidden life in God. There is no getting around this. You can get "jump starts" and impartations from other people, but to truly grow in supernatural dimensions, there will come a time to shut the door to distractions, busyness, and even good opportunities. The bigger your sphere of influence and anointing on your life, the more you will need a high level of discernment to choose multiplied opportunities. The only means of getting to that higher level of discernment is to shut the door for a while and maintain a private life with God. In order for you to go through the new doors I am putting in front of you, you must do what you used to do that got you to where you are today. He was telling me to maintain what I had attained. Now, for me, one of those spiritual disciplines was praying in the gift of tongues. Years ago, the Holy Spirit caught me like a fish on a hook, and He knew what bait to use. He asked me, "Do you want to hear God?" I said, "Yes." Then He responded, "If you will pray in the Spirit for two hours in one setting, I will give you the spirit of revelation."

Once inside, the widow was to "pour out" her oil into the vessels that she had borrowed. We are to "pour out" the anointing we have received into the "vessels" we have brought into our inner place. We are not to hoard our anointing. Elisha told the woman to pour it out, not hold it back. The more we give away our anointing, the more we receive and the more it multiplies in others lives.

The filled vessels were to be set aside; those "vessels" into whom we pour our anointing will be sanctified. Just like us, they will become so "ruined" for God that they will be of earthly good. They will be so filled up that they *will* become history makers and history changers. Oh Lord, raise up a generation of "set apart ones" who freely receive and freely give away!

After Elisha gave the widow her instructions, she was quick and faithful to carry them out. She received the Word, and then she obeyed the Word. Obedience is probably the most important key of all because without it none of the preceding steps will matter. Moving in supernatural flow requires simple, trusting obedience. If you want to receive more, be faithful and obedient with what little you have.

Like some of the seasoned seers I knew, I used to grunt, groan, sweat, and strain in the hopes of getting a highly detailed word of knowledge. In trying to be like them, I was undercutting what the Lord was giving me. Learning from others is great. But comparing yourself to others is one of the biggest pitfalls to avoid.

Matthew's Gospel tells of a Canaanite woman who asked Jesus to heal her daughter. In testing her, Jesus replied that it was "not good to take the children's bread and throw it to the dogs." The woman then answered, "Yes, Lord, but even the dogs feed on the crumbs which fall from their master's table" (Matt. 15:26-27).

When the widow finished filling all her vessel, the oil stopped flowing. In the supernatural realm, the anointing continues to flow until all available vessels are filled, or all the appointed needs are met. The flow ceases when there are no more vessels left to fill.

The final principle from the story of Elisha and the widow deals with where we are today in the move of God. Elisha told the widow to take her vessels of oil out of the house, sell them, and then to pay off her debt and live on the rest.

Our anointing is not only to be used by those who are in the "house" with us. We must go beyond our door, give what we have into the world and release it into the marketplace or wherever else a need exists. God's heart is so big that He wants us to share our anointing with others and prosper as well. In every facet of life, He wants us to move in the supernatural dimension.

Matthew 26:26-28 And as they were eating, Jesus took bread, and blessed *it,* and brake *it,* and gave *it* to the disciples, and said, Take, eat; this is my body. And he took the cup, and gave thanks, and gave *it* to them, saying, Drink ye all of it; For this is my blood of the new testament, which is shed for many for the remission of sins.

If you want to move in the supernatural, love the Cross, the blood and passion of Jesus, and also love His body, the Church.

What does God want to do with your life? He wants you to impact people, cities, and nations with His supernatural abundance. He wants you to stand in the light and let a shadow be cast from your life onto someone else's. Stand in the light. Walk in the light. Love the light of God. I guarantee you that His shadow will fall from a person who knows Him. Let the shadow of His supernatural presence fall in Jesus' great name.

# Chapter Six

# Pursuing an Encounter With God

This Chapter pretty much can sum-up the reason for this book A Scripture passage may specifically reference the great day of the Lord's second coming, it also applies to different times of divine visitation to mankind throughout history. During such divine encounters, the manifested presence of God literally comes into our "time-space world" to invade our unholy comfort zones with His glory. In those moments, the limits of passing time and our three-dimensional, physical world fall to the wayside as the Creator of time—who fills and maintains all things—turns that world upside-down. His coming radically shifts our old paradigms to reveal eternal aspects of His personality, character, power, and loveliness. Yet, even more so, God comes in times of divine visitation to reveal Himself. Whether God reveals Himself to individuals (or entire generations) throughout the course of unfolding Church history, those times of visitation will forever change people—if we let them. They have certainly changed our lives! When God enters the front stage of our existence, our favorite defining statement becomes: "We're not who we were, we're not who we want to be, and we're not yet who we're going to be." We are all in the process of being changed from glory to glory, because the Holy Spirit's purpose is to mold us into the likeness of Christ. Because of the new birth, we are no longer who we once were, and, because of His resurrection, we are destined to become more than we are now. First John 3:2 says, "Beloved, now we are children of God, and it has not appeared as yet what we will be. We know that when He appears, we will be like Him, because we will see Him just as He is." We are destined to become like Jesus.

Our transformation into His likeness is a process that occurs over time—the entire span of our Christian lives, in fact. Per-haps that is one reason why the Bible refers to the journey as a *walk:* "We walk by faith, not by sight" (2 Cor. 5:7); we "walk in newness of life" (Rom. 6:4); we "walk by the Spirit" (Gal. 5:16); we "walk in love" (Eph. 5:2); we "walk in the Light" (1 John 1:7); we "[walk] in the truth" (3 John 3); as we have "received Christ Jesus the Lord," so we "walk in Him" (Col. 2:6). The more we walk with the Lord, the more the Spirit changes us into His likeness.

All over the world, many different branches of the Church are discovering the need for certain giftings that have been silenced for a long time. Some of our current leaders, who are strong in their gifts and positions, are accustomed to being the "chief mouthpiece of God" to their churches. At times, they are so used to talking that they just keep on talking and talking, and do so long after God has gone home. They find security in hearing their own voice.

The Church is in transition right now, and many of us will have to learn how to give and take under the Holy Spirit's direction. Too many people in the Body of Christ are out of place and out of joint. Yes, great gifting is alive and active in their lives, but they are frustrated because the God-life within them has been constricted in little man-made boxes. Too many times, we have placed narrow, rigid, man-made definitions on God-made gifts and—like oil and water—the two never mix. When limited definitions are promoted as "God-inspired" job descriptions, the people God has anointed with supernatural gifts are forced to function within politically correct definitions. But change is on the horizon. In this generation, the Lord is releasing a wider spectrum of His presence to His people. The Holy Spirit is whetting our taste buds with new avenues of expressing His power and love. Untold thousands of people with revelatory gifts are sitting in church pews, attending Sunday school classes, and singing in services, but their heavenly gifts have been muted. Low expectations, limited understandings, and personal fears have squelched their releasing prophetic gifts. But God is ready to open the door because a harvest is coming. He is raising up a heavenly song destined to go far beyond the Church's four walls. For authentic change to arrive, this wonderful prophetic presence must invade the world's marketplace. It is time for prophetic evangelism—the harvest is upon us!

Existing leaders in the Body of Christ must recognize where God's anointing is resting in the days to come. I believe that God's anointing is going to come from some places that we would never have expected. But this is not a new wonder—just look at where Jesus tapped the anointing: in rough fishermen at the seashore; in despised tax collectors; in religious fanatics who advocated Rome's violent overthrow; and in the same religious seminary setting where His enemies ordered His crucifixion, as later seen in the Lord's choice of Saul, who was the star pupil of Israel's top-ranking Pharisee, Gamaliel. None of the Lord's disciples would have been invited to speak at most of today's churches; they did not have degrees, pedigrees, or social standing. If we want to tap the anointings of Peter, Paul, James, and John that are lying dormant in our churches, then it will take discerning eyes to see them, and secure leaders full of grace to make room for them.

Over the years, we have dealt with countless issues that required radical change in our lives. We're still dealing with issues of change, as are you and the Church around the world. The visitations we received had nothing to do with our personal agenda, pride, or sense of self. We believe that the Lord was giving us a precursor of what He wanted to do with His Bride, the Body of Christ.

We need to commit to this journey into intimacy with God and "take the intimacy plunge."

The Gospel of John offers a glimpse of our appearance on this path of God: "The wind blows where it wishes and you hear the sound of it, but do not know where it comes from and where it is going; so is everyone who is born of the Spirit" (John 3:8).

The Lord wants to blow away all the self-imposed controls that have entangled our lives. He wants to blow away our fear of men, our fear of breaking traditions, and our fear of repercussions. He wants us to be all that He has planned for us to be.


Song of Solomon 5:6 I opened to my beloved; but my beloved had withdrawn himself, *and* was gone: my soul failed when he spake: I sought him, but I could not find him; I called him, but he gave me no answer.


Song of Solomon 5:8 I charge you, O daughters of Jerusalem, if ye find my beloved, that ye tell him, that I *am* sick of love.


The Lord has given us invitation after invitation to come into a place of intimacy with Him. This is a place where you must press in for Him. You do so because He is pressing in toward you at the same time. The mystery of the gospel is the mystery of a divine, eternal love story—it is all about capturing our hearts and wooing us into the place where nothing matters except being in unbroken fellowship with God. Walking in the Spirit has little to do with only head knowledge; it has everything to do with a heart response of knowing that your Bridegroom is calling. God is calling for His Bride, and He is fighting for His Bride. He ardently loves His Bride, and He is asking us to be mirrors of His perfect image, which is Himself. He longs for us to be valiant warriors for His sake, and be people so in love with Him that no cost is too great!

I have a word for you—it is simple, yet profound and clear. Our God is a God of love, strength, and power. His great desire is toward you—His beloved Bride. Yes, pursue the God of visitation, and not the visitations of God. Seek the God of power, and not just the power of God.

Pursue the God of encounters! But keep first things first. When He grants you extraordinary encounters, remember that their ultimate purpose is to reveal the person of Jesus Christ, to bring you into a greater intimacy with the Father, and empower you to testify to others of His great love!


Hosea 6:1-3 Come, and let us return unto the LORD: for he hath torn, and he will heal us; he hath smitten, and he will bind us up. After two days will he revive us: in the third day he will raise us up, and we shall live in his sight. Then shall we know, *if* we follow on to know the LORD: his going forth is prepared as the morning; and he shall come unto us as the rain, as the latter *and* former rain unto the earth.

Now is the time for us to pursue the God of our visitation, and for His latter rain to water the earth. When you really love someone, and your heart for them is sold out 100 percent, then there is nothing you wouldn't do for your beloved. No task is too difficult. Knowing Him is the ultimate goal of all God encounters. The more you receive, the more you have to give away! It is time for us to give our all for Him who gave His all for us. Let us pursue the God of visitations and may close encounters with a supernatural God be yours! You too can be changed by the prophetic power of the supernatural!

# Chapter Seven

# Revelation of Jesus Christ Unveiled

One of my greatest revelations for me personally was that Jesus is the core of true presence. If you have a passion for Jesus Christ, the Presence of God will truly be there too. The word *revelation* means to lift the veil. We all need more of it. However, revelation has received a weird vibe because of flakey people who do not understand it.

If we are truly going to experience an increase of God's presence and power in our lives, we must receive revelation. In no way do I mean going beyond the Bible or becoming extra-biblical. God has given us His Holy Spirit without measure. He will never contradict His Word. He will, however, contradict your opinion of His Word. Consider the great evangelists and revivalists of yesterday.

Men like Jonathan Edwards, and John Wesley were among those whom God used to bring an awakening—a God-consciousness—to society. When these men preached, they spoke of a "new conversion experience" in the light of being born again. When they preached and the Word of God went forth, many people prayed and fasted for days, and sometimes weeks, until they experienced a sense of "release." Only then did they feel like they were truly saved. This is a far cry from today. We know and understand that whosoever calls upon the name of the Lord shall be saved. Period! We understand that salvation comes through grace—the grace bestowed on us when Jesus died on the cross and paid the price for it. We do not have to pay for it again. But these believers were not wrong. They simply were operating under the revelation they had at that time. Now we can see how that revelation has grown. The same can be said about divine healing. In the early days, people believed that through faith they could see people healed in their bodies. But many also believed that God put sickness on people. They had an Old Testament understanding of God's nature. We understand today that sickness comes from sin and as the result of many roots. But either way, God's mercy and love will always desire to heal. Whether healing takes place or not, the nature of God is never negated.

Today we can see how revelation has grown in various ways. The early church believed that tongues were the initial and only evidence of the infilling of the Holy Ghost. Now, we clearly see that is not the case. Tongues are one evidence, but not the only evidence, of being filled with the Spirit.

Jesus did not say, "You will receive tongues after the Holy Ghost comes upon you." That's just foolish. He said, "You will receive power..." (see Acts 1:8).

Jesus continued, "...and you shall be My witnesses..." The reason we receive power is to be a witness! The indwelling of the Holy Ghost is evidenced by boldness, power, presence, and many other factors.

1 Peter 1:7 That the trial of your faith, being much more precious than of gold that perisheth, though it be tried with fire, might be found unto praise and honour and glory at the appearing of Jesus Christ:

Here is the key to revelation: it is Jesus Christ! If we desire revelation, then we need to understand that it will be the revelation of Jesus. We cannot seek or get revelation any other way; it is of Jesus Christ. Many people think revelation is "goose bumps" or even a hyped service. They are sadly mistaken. Trust me, not many people are actually receiving biblical revelation. Many are just people who chase feelings. They feed off an earthly lust of attention, and their lives seldom produce fruit.

Everyone with an ounce of truth can see and discern this. It is these folks who hurt and set back the Body of Christ. As long as we continue to tolerate shallow believers who have never been changed by the power of God, we are in trouble. We need more. We need revelation. But it must be of Jesus Christ. If we think that we have seen and understand all of who Jesus is, we are deceived. This gift of life we have been given in Christ is an invitation to more.

What if I gave you a car, a BMW? Let's say I walked into your house and gave it to you as a gift. I just handed you the keys and told you that it was right outside. Then you picked up the phone and told everyone you knew that you had received this gift. That would be awesome. However, if I revisited your home a few weeks later only to find out that you had never walked out of the house and gotten in your car that would be a problem. Imagine I stopped by a few years later only to discover that you indeed went outside, opened the door, and drove the car—but only around your parking lot. Even if you were satisfied and content, at the end of the day, you had still never really operated the car. If I gave you a

BMW and after years and years you had only managed to drive it a few feet, that would be frustrating. Here I gave you a nice car, and you have never experienced what it can do! Of course, our Father in Heaven is no earthly man, and He does not get frustrated. However, we have been given a gift from God that we have not yet fully opened. For years we have been taught how to operate something that few people fully operate.

1 Peter 1:3-5 Blessed *be* the God and Father of our Lord Jesus Christ, which according to his abundant mercy hath begotten us again unto a lively hope by the resurrection of Jesus Christ from the dead, To an inheritance incorruptible, and undefiled, and that fadeth not away, reserved in heaven for you, Who are kept by the power of God through faith unto salvation ready to be revealed in the last time.

There is a "ready to be revealed" salvation awaiting us! Of course, we are saved. Of course, we are born again. But there is more the Father wants to show us.

We have not fully seen what the true expression of this gift is. It's not that God is hiding it away. It is that we have not understood the gift and are blind. There is such a great salvation we still need to experience. Jesus did not die on the cross so that we can go to church.

Jesus did not die so that we can live a partial life of victory and blessing. We need to experience all that God has for us.

Hosea 4:6 **My people are destroyed for lack of knowledge**: because thou hast rejected knowledge, I will also reject thee, that thou shalt be no priest to me: seeing thou hast forgotten the law of thy God, I will also forget thy children.

We need to understand why a lack of knowledge, or vision, can and will cause us to perish. How can someone be destroyed simply by living an unfruitful and barren life here on earth? Many people today have become comfortable living below the level of awareness God has called them to. If we come to Christianity and simply play a part-time role, never experiencing victory, we have just traded one form of bondage for another. Because of a lack of freedom and victory, we get into a mindset that desires escape. We think a victorious life is not for us. But the greatest years of our lives are ahead of us! We will finish and do all that God has for us to do. We simply need vision! We need revelation! That's what will enable us to finish strong. One may ask, "Why do we need revelation when the doctrines have been established and set?" Revelation is not creating doctrine; revelation is allowing us to live the doctrine we believe. Getting Out of the Natural We see an example of this in the Book of John.

John 4 tells us that Jesus met a woman at Jacob's well. When He walked up to the woman by the well, He graced her and made the most powerful statement: *"Give Me a drink"* ( John 4:7).

John 4:9 Then saith the woman of Samaria unto him, **How is it that thou, being a Jew, askest drink of me, which am a woman of Samaria?** for the Jews have no dealings with the Samaritans.

In the time of Jesus, Jews had no dealings with Samaritans. This is the first opportunity this woman missed. Here was Jesus, the most powerful man—God in the flesh—who has ever lived.

He speaks a few words, and people are healed, delivered, and raised from the dead. He asked this lady for a drink, though He clearly was not thirsty. He was giving her an opportunity to receive freedom and to understand who she truly was. Jesus was initiating the opportunity of a lifetime. The multitudes flocked to Him, but here He was coming to her. Obviously, this is her first chance to understand, and she didn't get it. She reverted to the natural.

John 4:10 Jesus answered and said unto her, If thou knewest the gift of God, and who it is that saith to thee, Give me to drink; thou wouldest have asked of him, and he would have given thee living water.

So Jesus, in His love and mercy, told her, essentially, "I am not here for a natural encounter; I am here for a deeper cause." And she responded:

John 4:11 The woman saith unto him, Sir, thou hast nothing to draw with, and the well is deep: from whence then hast thou that living water?

Here is the second missed opportunity for freedom. Jesus was not talking about water. There is no Jesus beverage called "living water." At that moment, she really believed that He was offering her a beverage! So Jesus, in His love and mercy, kept going—trying to give her a chance for freedom.

John 4:13, 14 Jesus answered and said unto her, Whosoever drinketh of this water shall thirst again: But whosoever drinketh of the water that I shall give him shall never thirst; but the water that I shall give him shall be in him a well of water springing up into everlasting life.

Jesus made it clear as day that He was not there for natural reasons. He even went as far as saying that this natural water would not satisfy and that what He had to give would eternally satisfy. He also mentioned that something would happen on the inside of her. He could not have been more clear!

John 4:15 The woman saith unto him, Sir, give me this water, that I thirst not, neither come hither to draw.

Here is the third missed opportunity. Jesus was not talking about the natural. But she kept on bringing up the natural. In the same way, we cannot continue to approach a supernatural God naturally. We will miss what the Lord is trying to tell us. Thank God that Jesus was loving and patient and saw her heart and decided to keep speaking to her.

John 4:16 Jesus saith unto her, Go, call thy husband, and come hither.

Jesus decided to speak into her past, revealing secrets no one knew.

John 4:17 The woman answered and said, I have no husband. Jesus said unto her, Thou hast well said, I have no husband:

Here is the fourth missed opportunity. Jesus did not speak in the natural to her at any time during their conversation. But she kept speaking in the flesh. Scripture is filled with nonbelievers who heard one word from Christ and were changed, and this woman missed four opportunities for her life to be changed. Christ now made it personal. He decided to touch on an area few knew about. After she said she didn't have a husband, Christ began to prophetically open up her heart by revealing five husbands in her past and a current messed up relationship. After practically hearing Jesus bring her whole past life before her, she missed yet another opportunity.

John 4:19, 20 The woman saith unto him, Sir, I perceive that thou art a prophet. Our fathers worshipped in this mountain; and ye say, that in Jerusalem is the place where men ought to worship.

This is a valuable lesson regarding how revelation operates. Many times Christ will try to speak truth that would set us free. But we are stuck on what we have always known and cannot or chose not to hear. Our measuring stick for the future cannot be the lack we have seen in the past. In this hour, Jesus is speaking more clearly than He ever has, and many of us continue to revert to that which we have always known. The danger in such a pattern is that when Christ comes to give us revelation, truth that will add to what we are operating in, we cannot continue to operate under what we already know.

The Bible is a guidebook for living a meaningful life—a life of power and love. We cannot continue to say we believe in the Word of God yet not live it out. Jesus must alter our human-made doctrines and theologies so that we can live His Word. Many of us have been stuck in institutionalized Christianity and have had our ability to understand truth stolen from us. Jesus Himself said He was the way, the truth, and the life (see John 14:6). Yet we continue to settle for people's regurgitated doctrine of devils, while Jesus is offering a better way. I remember when I was first born again and saw folks praying for the sick. This is difficult for many believers today because they do not operate in biblical authority. The Word of God is our final authority. If we do not see a biblical pattern at least three times throughout Scripture, then we have no business creating a doctrine out of something.

In the Book of Galatians, we see Paul addressing a few churches regarding false doctrinal issues. The elders in some of these churches were rising up and saying Paul's Gospel message was not valid.

Galatians 1:11, 12 But I certify you, brethren, that the gospel which was preached of me is not after man. For I neither received it of man, neither was I taught *it,* but by the revelation of Jesus Christ.

Paul addressed this concern by saying his message did not come by people; it came by a revelation of Jesus Christ. We need a revelation of Jesus Christ. It is not what is in His hands; it is Him. I do not look at Jesus Christ as separate from miracles and power. The source is all the same. When we receive Christ, everything that Christ is and represents is in us. We must continue to seek the truth that will set us free.

If we really find value in the Bible, then we must be willing to learn who Jesus is and learn His ways. It's time that the veil over our heads and hearts is removed! I believe that you will walk in the fullness of Jesus as He reveals more of His nature to you.

# Chapter Eight
# Revival Outpouring

R evival Outpouring is promised in the Word of God. He promised that He would pour out His Spirit upon all flesh. There's an invitation tonight. Cities all over the world, I believe the Lord is speaking. I know the Lord is speaking from John Chapter 1. Stay in an attitude of worship for a moment as we bring a word from heaven.

The Lord's been speaking to me about visitation and habitation-about being a resting place for the presence of the Lord. God is looking and knocking at the door of the heart. Whoever opens up that door, Jesus will come in and dine with them and they will dine with Him. How many of you know the Lord is knocking?

The Lord is looking for someone. He's looking for a city, or a nation, a church, or a ministry. There's an invitation. I'm prophesying and talking about visitation and habitation tonight.

I was meditating on John Chapter 1, beginning in verse 35, "Again, the next day, John stood with two of his disciples. 36 And looking at Jesus as He walked, he said, "Behold the Lamb of God!" The two disciples heard him speak, and they followed Jesus. Then Jesus turned, and seeing them following, said to them, "What do you seek? They said to Him, "Rabbi" (which is to say, when translated, Teacher), "where are You staying?" He said to them, "Come and see." An invitation-Jesus said "Come and see." "Where are You staying Teacher? Where's the place of habitation? Where's the place where the Son of Man lays His head? Where's the place of the outpouring of glory and power?" And Jesus says, "Come and see." And then the Scripture says, they came and saw where He was staying and remained with Jesus that day.

It just struck me, pierced my heart, that is what I want. I want to see where Jesus is staying. I want an invitation into the place of habitation-hosting the presence of God. The Lord is saying, "What is it that you're seeking?" And they responded, "Where are You staying?" And Jesus said, "Come and see." And they came and saw and stayed with Jesus. Not visitation, but habitation. Not just blessing. I want to be in the place where Jesus is staying. I want to be the place where I can host the presence of God.

Psalms 27:4 One *thing* have I desired of the LORD, that will I seek after; that I may dwell in the house of the LORD all the days of my life, to behold the beauty of the LORD, and to enquire in his temple.

What are you seeking? What are you looking for? I'm looking for the place where Jesus is. I'm looking for the place where Jesus is staying. I'm looking for the place of habitation. I don't just want a visitation-I'm talking about hosting the presence of God. I'm talking about the rest of God. One thing I desire and one thing I will seek, that I will dwell in the house of the Lord forever.

Luke 9:58 And Jesus said unto him, Foxes have holes, and birds of the air *have* nests; but the Son of man hath not where to lay *his* head.

Jesus is looking for somewhere-a church, a ministry, a city, a people-to lay His head. The Son of Man is looking for a home. The Son of Man is looking for habitation. "Where are You staying Jesus? Show me the place You are staying." And Jesus said, "Come and see. Come and see the place that I'm staying. Come and see My habitation." "What is it that you're seeking?" "The place where You're staying." Come and see, and they stayed with Jesus that day. I'm talking about hosting the presence of God because foxes have holes and birds in the air have nests, but the Son of Man has nowhere to lay His head, and He's looking.

Could it be your church altar? Could it be your ministry altar? Right now? Son of Man, come and make Your home in me. How hungry are you?

Prophesying and talking about visitation and habitation reminded me of Luke Chapter 24. It's a word of the Lord. You may remember the story of the two disciples on the road to Emmaus.

Luke 24:28 And they drew nigh unto the village, whither they went: and he made as though he would have gone further.

They came to the place where two friends on the road say goodbye to one another and go in one direction and Jesus goes in another. The Scripture says Jesus indicated, He acted like, He was going to go to another city. He was bringing the blessing and the visitation, and He was going to another city. The Bible says something amazing in verse 29:

Luke 24:29 But they constrained him, saying, Abide with us: for it is toward evening, and the day is far spent. And he went in to tarry with them.

We see the same thing in John Chapter 1. "What is it that you're seeking?" "Where are You staying?" And Jesus said "Come and see." And they stayed with Him that day. In the example of Jesus walking on the road with the two disciples, He acted like He was going to go on a little bit further. It was like a test. Knocking at the door of the heart. How hungry are you? How hungry are you Illinois? How hungry are you? Do you want Me to come and stay for a little while and then move on, or do you want to constrain Me? Constrain Me saying, "Abide with us. Don't go Jesus. Make Your home in me." They constrained Jesus means they laid ahold of Him aggressively, even violently. They said, "Don't go. We don't want visitation, we want habitation."

The only thing that can keep the presence of the Lord in an outpouring of revival is hunger. The Holy Spirit wants hunger. There's a hunger in this place. There's a hunger stirring. There's a hunger rising. You're saying, "Don't pass me by." You're saying, "Come Holy Spirit." You're saying "Come into the altar of my heart, the altar of my church and ministry, the altar of my city." And God is saying, "Get ready." I am prophesying to cities and nations around the world. You can say, "God, one thing I desire, one thing I seek, that I will dwell in the house of the Lord." We can lift up our voices right now and say, "I want to see, I want to see the place where Jesus is staying. I want to be the place that's hosting."

It's an equal opportunity. The Son of Man is looking for a place to rest His head. The Son of Man is looking for a home. He doesn't just want to visit one City; He wants to abide. He doesn't just want to visit your church and your city; He wants to abide. He's looking for a dwelling place. He's looking for a host, someone that will host His presence-that will host the arch of His presence. He's looking for someone that would be hungry and say, "God, one thing I desire and one thing I seek, that I will dwell in the house of the Lord forever. I want to know the place, the place of revival, the place of blessing, the place of outpouring, the place of miracles, the place of harvest. I don't want to know the place of religion and tradition. I don't want to know the place that's dry and thirsty. I want to know where the Son of Man is. I want the Son of Man to find a home in me. I want Him to find a home in my church and find a home in my city and my nation." There's an opportunity tonight. An invitation. Not just visitation, but habitation.

Jesus wept over Jerusalem because they did not know their hour of visitation. How many cities did not know their hour of visitation? How many cities and nations right now do not know their hour of visitation? God is knocking at the door of your heart. How many of you are going to open the door? Wherever you're at, you can have revival. Wherever you're watching tonight, you can have an outpouring. It's not just for Illinois. It's not just for Belleville, but God is offering an outpouring. God wants hunger and people are hungry right now. They are like the disciples on the road to Emmaus, saying, "Jesus I don't want You just to come and bless. I want You to stay. I want You to stay in my house. I want the Son of Man to find a place to lay His head. I want to see the place where You're staying."

In the Spirit there's an opportunity for someone to grab a hold of a revival mantle and the move of God will begin to happen in your church. The move of God will begin to happen in your city. The move of God will begin to happen in your nation.

We can lift up our hands and say, "God, give me a double portion of the grace to have revival outpouring. Break out on a global scale, on a mass scale, all over the world, in living rooms around the world." It's your hunger right now. It's a moment right now. Come on in your living rooms. Get a hold of the word of the Lord. Say, "My God, I'm going to start a fire. My God, I'm going to start a fire. I'm going to start a fire. I want a mantle. I want a mantle to see revival in my city, in my nation, in my church. Start a fire."

**There is currently a fresh Healing Awakening and season of Revival on earth. Let's become His resting place and ask him to find His place with us and receive His Revival Outpouring.**

# Chapter Nine

# The Blessing of Obedience

I have taught more teachings in 2013 on obedience that in my entire ministry. GOD GIVES HIS HOLY SPIRIT TO THOSE WHO OBEY HIM (ACTS 5:32).

At this point we now turn our focus to the wonderful blessings of obedience. This will be most enjoyable. Yes, there is suffering in obeying God, but it does not compare with the blessings of obedience! This was the reason why the imprisoned Paul and Silas could sing hymns in the night (Acts 16:25). They saw beyond their hardship and glimpsed the glory.

More than one book could be written just expounding the benefits of walking in obedience to God. As you have seen, this was not the direction God had for this book. Though we will cover some benefits, you are destined to discover a multitude through your continued study and experiences in Christ.

I believe God's mandate for this book was instruction and warning— instruction on how to walk in obedience and warning to keep from deception. Instruction and warning are more crucial than the outlining of the benefits, for when you walk in the counsel and wisdom of God, you automatically experience the benefits, even if you are unaware of them. Conversely, you could know all the benefits and never receive them if you are not grounded in God's instruction and warning.

Luke 17:5, 6 And the apostles said unto the Lord, Increase our faith. And the Lord said, If ye had faith as a grain of mustard seed, ye might say unto this sycamine tree, Be thou plucked up by the root, and be thou planted in the sea; and it should obey you.

This illustrates that faith is given to each and every believer as a mustard seed. It is the kingdom principle of seedtime and harvest. "The kingdom of God is as if a man should scatter seed on the ground" (Mark 4:26). When we were saved we were assigned a measure of faith (Rom. 12:3). This faith is in seed form.

The apostles asked the Lord to increase their faith. But from what He is about to show them we learn it is our responsibility to increase our faith. Listen to this parable He uses to explain how to increase our faith:

Luke 17:7-9 But which of you, having a servant plowing or feeding cattle, will say unto him by and by, when he is come from the field, Go and sit down to meat? And will not rather say unto him, Make ready wherewith I may sup, and gird thyself, and serve me, till I have eaten and drunken; and afterward thou shalt eat and drink? Doth he thank that servant because he did the things that were commanded him? I trow not.

This parable always puzzled me. Why did Jesus go from comparing faith to a seed over to a servant plowing, tending sheep, and making dinner for his master? I did not understand until the morning God revealed it to me.

First, let's remember what question He is answering by this parable. It could be paraphrased, "How do we increase this seed of faith?" Next, examine the major focus of the parable. It represents the obedience of a servant toward his master. Referring to the servant's actions Jesus said, "He did the things that were commanded him."

A servant is responsible to carry out completely the will of his master, not just a portion or a sampling of it. It represents taking a task from start to completion. How often do many people begin a project or assignment never to finish it because they lost interest or because the labor and suffering became too intense? The true and faithful servant completes the project. He not only works the fields, but he also brings the fruit of his labor to his master and prepares the meal. This represents true obedience.

Let's recall two very important points.

1.    We must grow spiritually in the grace of God.

2.    We grow through obedience!


So how does this seed of faith grow in our hearts? By now you probably know the answer—by obedience—not partial and occasional obedience but obedience performed faithfully and diligently. Look closely at what Jesus went on to say.


Luke 17:10 So likewise ye, when ye shall have done all those things which are commanded you, say, We are unprofitable servants: we have done that which was our duty to do.

His answer emphasizes two aspects of increasing faith. First, obedience to completion: "when you have done all those things which you are commanded." Second, humility toward God: "We are unprofitable servants. We have done what was our duty to do."

Obedience is not obedience until we have completed all that we have been told to do. In addition, our posture of humility keeps us in His grace. Both of these things foster an atmosphere for faith to grow. Jesus used this parable to explain that faith increases as we submit to God's authority. The greater our submission to God, the greater our faith!

Jesus is teaching His disciples, "Pursue true humility, which will keep you in the grace of God. That grace will give you the ability to walk in obedience. By submitting to God's authority and walking in complete obedience your faith will increase."

Then the Holy Spirit reminded me of the Roman centurion who came to Jesus for help (Matt. 8). I quickly turned in my Bible to read this account afresh. As Jesus entered Capernaum, a centurion came to Him, pleading for Jesus to heal his servant who was at home in bed, paralyzed and racked with pain.

"Yes," Jesus said, "I will come and heal him."

But the centurion restrained Him by saying, "Lord, I am not worthy that You should come under my roof. But only speak a word, and my servant will be healed." Now read carefully why this soldier could say this to Jesus.


Matthew 8:9 For I am a man under authority, having soldiers under me: and I say to this *man,* Go, and he goeth; and to another, Come, and he cometh; and to my servant, Do this, and he doeth *it.*

This Roman soldier had a greater understanding of authority and obedience than most. He knew that those who were submitted to authority could be entrusted authority of their own. He was saying to Jesus, "I recognize You're a man under God's authority just as I am under the governing authority of my commanding officer. Because I obey my commander, I have been entrusted with those under my authority. Therefore, I have but to say one word, and the soldiers under me instantly obey."

He understood Jesus' source of authority. He recognized that Jesus' authority came from God. He knew Jesus was totally submitted to the Father. He knew this meant that all Jesus needed to do was speak a word and the devils who tormented his servant had to obey. Notice Jesus' response to this man's understanding of submission to authority.

Matthew 8:10 When Jesus heard *it,* he marvelled, and said to them that followed, Verily I say unto you, I have not found so great faith, no, not in Israel.

Notice Jesus linked directly faith and submission. This Roman soldier displayed greater faith than anyone in Israel because of his honor, respect, and submission to authority.

The centurion said, "All you have to do is speak a word and the tormentor will leave." Now tie this in with what Jesus said to the disciples who desired increased faith: "If you have faith as a mustard seed, you can say to this mulberry tree, 'Be pulled up by the roots and be planted in the sea,' and it would obey you" (Luke 17:6). Notice Jesus said all you have to do is speak a word and the tree will obey you! Who does this mulberry tree obey? The one who "did the things that were commanded him" (Luke 17:9–10).

71

I have watched believers who were rebellious to God's authority have a rough time. They are either barely making it or fighting to survive, not just in finances but in all areas—their marriage, children, Christian walk, and so on. They talk a good talk and may even pray fervently, yet deep down they wonder why their faith is not stronger. It is evident their faith is weak because they are afraid to submit to God's authority.

I also have witnessed submitted believers who possessed simple yet great faith. They usually do not stand out, for they are humble. Yet their words ring with the authority of heaven, and when things are rough, they shine bright.

We are required to live by faith, for "without faith it is impossible to please Him. For by it the elders obtained a good testimony" (Heb. 11:6, 2). Just like these elders of old, we receive the promises of God through faith and patience (Heb. 6:12). The greater our faith, the greater the capacity for us to receive God's promise. Our faith increases as our obedience continues.

We see this in the life of Abraham.

**Hebrews 11:17 By faith Abraham, when he was tried, offered up Isaac: and he that had received the promises offered up his only begotten *son,***

Abraham's obedience was complete. He did not reason himself out of obeying God's command. He did not procrastinate but rose early the morning after receiving the command. He undertook a difficult three-day journey to God's appointed place. Then he bound his son and lifted his knife, ready to slay his long-awaited promise.

While meditating on this God spoke to me, "Don't put Ishmael on the altar!" Ishmael was the son that Abraham conceived with Sarah's handmaiden, though the Lord had said earlier that Sarah would be the one to bear the promised son to Abraham. Ishmael represents what you have accomplished in your own strength. It is our attempt to bring to pass God's promise. Isaac represents the promise of God, the one you have waited and longed for. God will not ask for our Ishmael but for Isaac in His test of obedience.

After the angel of the Lord restrained Abraham from sacrificing his son, look what happens as a result of his obedience:

Genesis 22:13, 14 And Abraham lifted up his eyes, and looked, and behold behind *him* a ram caught in a thicket by his horns: and Abraham went and took the ram, and offered him up for a burnt offering in the stead of his son. And Abraham called the name of that place Jehovah jireh: as it is said *to* this day, In the mount of the LORD it shall be seen.

God revealed Himself in a new way to Abraham, *Jehovah-Jireh*. Abraham was the first to receive this revelation of God's character, which means: "Jehovah Sees."

God was not revealed to Abraham as "Jehovah Sees" until Abraham passed the test of obedience. There are many who claim to know the different characteristics of God's nature, yet they have never experienced obeying Him in the hard places. They may sing, "Jehovah Jireh, my provider," but it is a song from their heads not their hearts. They have yet to venture to the hard and arid place where He reveals Himself.

Not only did Abraham receive a fresh revelation of God's nature but he also secured, by his obedience, the promise God made to him. After he passed this test God told him:

Genesis 22:18 And in thy seed shall all the nations of the earth be blessed; because thou hast obeyed my voice.

This is quite a different outcome than the one experienced by his descendants who died in the wilderness. They too were given a promise, but they never received it because of their insubordinate hearts.

God continues to fulfill His promise to me. It always comes His way. With each step of obedience comes a new level of faith.

Obedience to our Father is the only way to go because of the following reasons:

1.    It honors Him with the glory He deserves.

2.    People's lives are truly changed.

3.    Obeying His will increases faith and develops character.

4.    It is the only source of life, joy, and peace. There awaits an eternal reward for our obedience.

5.    2 Corinthians 5:10  For we must all appear before the judgment seat of Christ; that every one may receive the things *done* in *his* body, according to that he hath done, whether *it be* good or bad.

This judgment is not of sinners but of believers. Notice Paul said, "good or bad." For those who obey God's will, "each one's work will become clear; for the Day will declare it, because it will be revealed by fire; and the fire will test each one's work, of what sort it is. If anyone's work which he has built on it endures, he will receive a reward" (1 Cor. 3:13–14).

Our God is a consuming fire (Heb. 12:29). He is the one who tests each of our works. Fire will burn and devour that which does not endure. It will purify and refine that which does. Our motives, intentions, and works will be revealed in His glorious light. Those who have obeyed with a pure heart will be rewarded. On the other hand:

1 Corinthians 3:15 If any man's work shall be burned, he shall suffer loss: but he himself shall be saved; yet so as by fire.

The way we will spend eternity is determined by our submission to His authority here. Nothing else matters, except to live a life of obedience to His will.

2 Peter 1:10, 11 Wherefore the rather, brethren, give diligence to make your calling and election sure: for if ye do these things, ye shall never fall: For so an entrance shall be ministered unto you abundantly into the everlasting kingdom of our Lord and Saviour Jesus Christ.

May the grace of our Lord Jesus Christ be with you both now and forever.

We can choose one of four responses when sin comes knocking.

1. Blatant disobedience

The way of disobedience is hard!

2. Reasoning yourself into disobedience

3. Obedience with a bad attitude

4. Obedience with a willing heart

# Author

Bill Vincent is no stranger to understanding the power of God. Not only has he spent over twenty years as a Minister with a strong prophetic anointing, he is now also an Apostle and Author with Revival Waves of Glory Ministries in Litchfield, IL. Along with his wife, Tabitha, he, leads a team providing apostolic oversight in all aspects of ministry, including service, personal ministry and Godly character.

Bill offers a wide range of writings and teachings from deliverance, to experiencing presence of God and developing Apostolic cutting edge Church structure. Drawing on the power of the Holy Spirit through years of experience in Revival, Spiritual Sensitivity, and deliverance ministry, Bill now focuses mainly on pursuing the Presence of God and breaking the power of the devil off of people's lives.

His books 48 and counting has since helped many people to overcome the spirits and curses of Satan. For more information or to keep up with Bill's latest releases, please visit www.revivalwavesofgloryministries.com. To contact Bill, feel free to follow him on twitter @revivalwaves.

# Recommended Books

## By Bill Vincent

Overcoming Obstacles

Glory: Pursuing God's Presence

Defeating the Demonic Realm

Increasing Your Prophetic Gift

Increase Your Anointing

Keys to Receiving Your Miracle

The Supernatural Realm

Waves of Revival

Increase of Revelation and Restoration

The Resurrection Power of God

Discerning Your Call of God

Apostolic Breakthrough

Glory: Increasing God's Presence

Love is Waiting – Don't Let Love Pass You By

The Healing Power of God

Glory: Expanding God's Presence

Receiving Personal Prophecy

Signs and Wonders

Signs and Wonders Revelations

Children Stories

The Rapture

The Secret Place of God's Power

Building a Prototype Church

Breakthrough of Spiritual Strongholds

Glory: Revival Presence of God

Overcoming the Power of Lust

Glory: Kingdom Presence of God

Transitioning to the Prototype Church

The Stronghold of Jezebel

Healing After Divorce

A Closer Relationship With God

Cover Up and Save Yourself

Desperate for God's Presence

The War for Spiritual Battles

Spiritual Leadership

Global Warning

Millions of Churches

Destroying the Jezebel Spirit

Awakening of Miracles

Deception and Consequences Revealed

Are You a Follower of Christ

Don't Let the Enemy Steal from You!

A Godly Shaking

The Unsearchable Riches of Christ

Heaven's Court System

Satan's Open Doors

Armed for Battle

The Wrestler

Spiritual Warfare: Complete Collection

Growing In the Prophetic

The Prototype Church: Complete Edition

Faith

The Angry Fighter's Story

Understanding Heaven's Court System

# Web Site:

www.revivalwavesofgloryministries.com

Lightning Source UK Ltd.
Milton Keynes UK
UKHW012230060223
416577UK00003B/332/J